Creative Bones

How creativity works. No, really.

D1738664

By GUY BOMMARITO

First Edition

ISBN-13: 978-0615998657

Cover design by Ken Shafer Design Inc. Designer: Ken Shafer.

To Mimi, Carisa, Brant, Marin, Zoe and Kyra. Yes, all of you. Because you are who you are. And because I don't think I'm going to write another book.

Preface

The purpose of this book is to knock the creative process off its mystical reserved-for-people-with-more-talent-in-their-pinky-fingers-than-the-rest-of-us-have-in-our-entire-bodies perch and make it accessible to anyone with half a mind to pursue better answers to pretty much every question out there — not unlike that TV show where a rogue magician reveals stage secrets behind well-known magic acts, much to the chagrin of his fellow wand wavers. (Spoiler alert: It's not really magic.)

That said, three types of people should benefit from this book. The first are those who make their living in a creative field but have never given much thought to, and really have no idea, how they do what they do. They only know that the deadline for their next big idea is Thursday at noon, and it better be good. For them, becoming aware of some of the things they do instinctively (on good days) should be more than interesting, it should alleviate a ton of angst. It did for me.

The second group for whom this book is written is what might be called "dabblers" — individuals who are often told how creative they are (by people other than their mothers) for doing things that they themselves might describe as the product of messing around. Lack of confidence, conviction and direction that would take their creative output to the next level has, regrettably, kept them from fully exploring their creative envelopes, much less pushing them. This book should unlock doors for these people that they thought were walls.

The final category of homo sapiens that should benefit from this book consists of people with no desire to create anything more elaborate than breakfast. Unfortunately, they live in a world where they are constantly being asked to think outside the box, to bring new thoughts to the table and "if you could have something on my desk by the end of the day, that would be great." These people don't really "get" creativity, but somewhere in the backs of their minds they wonder if some method of thinking not covered in high school might exist that would take them or their work or their lives to far more interesting and productive places. (Well yes, there is.)

First, two quick clarifications: While many of the insights on these pages come from my years as an advertising agency creative director and writer, this book is not about advertising. People in advertising may recognize some shared experiences, but that's about it.

This book is also not specifically about drawing or writing or redecorating living rooms or redesigning bridges or coming up with the next digital doohickey or totally reinventing industries, institutions and enterprises that leave the competition wondering if anyone got the number of the metaphorical semi that just hit them — unless any of those things happen to be what someone wants to do.

Then it's exactly about that.

Contents

Creative
Bones

Introduction

An advertising agency I worked for moved to new offices not long after I joined them. As might be expected, one of our first tasks was determining what to put on the walls. Along with the usual suspects — corporate graphics, work samples, awards — was the thought to take one wall and do something fun with it.

One suggestion everybody seemed to like was the idea of producing a series of custom-designed skateboard decks. The boards could be hung in two rows of ten down the main hallway, providing an entertaining counterpoint to the company signage and client logos in the lobby.

To broaden ownership of the project, everyone in the agency was invited to come up with ideas for designs.

A few weeks into the project, I ran into one of our IT guys in the elevator. He asked how submissions were coming. I happily responded that everyone from the creative department to accounting appeared to be contributing to the cause. Then, he said something that hit me as if I was hearing it for the first time, even though I'd heard it a thousand times before. "I'd love to participate," he said, "but I don't have a creative bone in my body."

This time, for some reason, the statement stuck in my

gut.

Here's the deal. Some people tap into creativity effortlessly. Others, don't. Yet, everyone can create to some level. The problem is, creativity comes with a mystique that leaves most people with the mistaken impression that only a chosen few have the "gift" for it.

Worse, people not only perceive creativity as something beyond their pay scales, they go about their lives literally avoiding, negating and discounting creative thinking, all for the very best of reasons — "reason" being chief among them.

So to get things started, tattoo this on your favorite body part:

Creativity has less to do with who you are than what you do.

Creative thinking is simply a way of looking at things, a way of solving problems, a way of coming up with thoughts that never occurs to or is outright rejected by most people because it's too silly, irrational or counterintuitive.

To further complicate matters, common definitions that rely on words like "imagination" and "originality" for illumination do little to clarify. Perhaps a better way to understand creativity is to think of it like this:

Creativity is nonsense that leads to a breakthrough.

Completely illogical. Frustratingly capricious. Contrary to common sense. Creativity, unlike most subjects, defies rational comprehension. As a result, it has proven uncharacteristically challenging for everyone from academics to artists to decipher in a meaningful way. (While creativity has been painstakingly analyzed, documented and discussed, right down to which hemisphere of the brain does what, few studies provide a useful guide to actually creating anything.)

It takes me back to something I learned when I was teaching a course on creativity at the University of Texas. Academia is exceptionally good at taking things apart, identifying every molecule and drawing conclusions. However, dissection and analysis are, at best, starting points to new and fresh — which explains why the talent for breaking down a poem or a novel isn't routinely reverse-engineered into acclaimed poetry and literature.

Poets never sit down to create a poem in iambic pentameter with a nice balance of metaphors, personifications and alliterations, and an onomatopoeia thrown in for good measure. (Or if they do, they write a really bad poem.) Poets have something to say and their poetry just happens to be the way it comes out. The more deliberate the poet, the more hackneyed the poem.

None of this is to imply any disrespect for the impressive body of scholarly work on creativity that exists today. Quite the contrary, it's simply to set the stage for providing a working knowledge of a subject that at its core is about things that don't make sense.

Until they make sense.

Chapter 1

Stupid equals smart.

While this book may read like a "how to" at times, the response from people instinctively comfortable with creative thinking is likely to be "I can't recall ever doing anything like that."

For the most part, creative people don't think about the process. Marshall McLuhan once said, "We don't know who discovered water, but we know it wasn't the fish." For creative people, same thing: Rarely are they aware of the mechanics behind what they do. Creative thinking is simply inherent to who they are.

So, for everyone else, here's the first and maybe most important rule in any creative endeavor: **Trust the method, even though every instinct may be screaming what a ridiculous and complete waste of time it is.**

If there's one obstacle to creativity for the rational thinker, that's it.

Delivering at the creative level takes an enormous amount of faith, drive and even courage. To start with, it's based on some highly irrational principles, if there even are such things. It's all completely paradoxical, and that's why it works. Think about it.

If creativity was logical, it would lead to the same places everyone has already been.

Creativity is about stumbling onto something new. (Just to be clear, the "stumbling" part is not an option.)

It's not so much about hard work, although it can take significant effort. It's about discovering the unexpected while playing around, intentionally or otherwise. It's not about getting everybody in a room to brainstorm ideas (more on that later). It's about the willingness to search for answers in random and completely illogical places. It's not about waiting for the muse to come. It's about realizing she already stopped by, and somebody wasn't paying attention.

The creative process is basically a series of mental meanderings that lead to unexpected thoughts, expressions or solutions. As such, successful creative outings require the willingness to entertain a broad range of totally unrelated material in a manner not unlike what our parents used to call "goofing off" — and to do so while that recording inside our heads with the voices of every teacher/boss/authority figure we've ever known is telling us to get back to work and do something productive.

It's less like traditional thinking than it is like choreographed falling.

Given our competitive ethic and nose-to-the-grindstone culture, i.e., "you're not working unless it looks like you're working," addressing important issues with what appears to be the inability to take them seriously represents a huge barrier for those who have never experienced the "Aha!" moment.

That's why, to succeed in any creative endeavor, trusting the process is paramount. That starts with understanding that creating is not the same as making widgets. It isn't about work in the traditional sense.

That kind of thinking will just add another set of footprints to the well-trodden path of "been there, done that," if it leads anywhere at all, and creativity is about going where no one has gone. That means giving up the dictum of following linear thoughts to logical conclusions.

If it helps, think of the creative process as permission to embrace one's inner stupid — because it's the only way to come up with something so incredibly smart that no one ever thought of it before.

Chapter 2

What Yoda said.

Let the force be with you.

Or, to be more precise, the force is already with you. Quit sending it back.

How much help does gravity need to do its job? How about hair growing? Exhaling? Or blinking?

Creativity is like that: a force of nature. It's when we "think" about it in the traditional sense that the process comes to a halt.

Creating is about allowing the self to be in the moment. (And if it weren't for that stupid inner voice that's always telling us what to do and what to think, we'd always be in the moment.)

As hard as that sounds, here's the good news. The process of creating is like an express train to nirvana. It's only when we start thinking about creating, when we think about what we're trying to do, when we try to create, that the ride goes off the rails.

Yogi Berra once said, "You can't think and play baseball at the same time." Creativity? Ditto.

Creativity is the self against logic and reality and common sense and the way things are supposed to be done. The only way to defeat all of the above is to take away the power we give those things to control our thoughts and actions.

In a vaguely related way, it's like meditation. Deliberately trying to shut out the world while contemplating "awareness" is maddening until finally mastered. It's only when we learn to stop trying that we succeed.

So, rule number two: Don't think, just do. Allow the moment to take care of itself once the creating begins.

Playtime

Without wading too deep into the right brain/left brain debate and pop culture's penchant for attributing various responsibilities to one hemisphere or the other, a noticeable mental shift occurs during any creative endeavor.

The easiest way to experience this change is to take out a pen and paper and draw a squiggly line down one side of the page. On the other side (at least six inches away), draw another squiggle — absolutely identical in every nuance and curve — so that, when complete, the two lines are mirror images of each other.

As the second line is being drawn, pay attention to the conscious shift that takes place from general awareness to what might be described as a sort of focused serenity. Remember that feeling. That's what being in the moment feels like, and it's as integral to the process as anything ever written about creativity. (In sports jargon, this state or feeling is not unlike "being in the zone.")

It's also a great way for people new to the creative process to assess whether they are having a bona fide creative moment or simply trying to have a bona fide creative moment.

The two are not the same.

Chapter 3

One down, 99 to go.

Creativity isn't as much about hard work as it is about a lot of work. Yes, some ideas serendipitously drop onto our mental doorsteps the moment we need them — sometimes before we're even looking for them. Those occasions are the exception.

The raw materials that lead to creative solutions come from the sum of our experiences. Every trip to the mall or flight to Italy represents another drop in the bucket of data available for answers to questions yet to be encountered. When we occasionally receive instant insights, it's because, in some form, the blueprints were already on file.

Years ago, I worked on a very challenging restaurant account. On one occasion, my creative team did a campaign that flopped so badly the client decided to fire our agency. Because this account represented a significant portion of our profits, we did the only prudent thing. We begged for a second chance. The marketing director responded by giving us one final opportunity to deliver, as long as what we delivered was a TV spot that took place in the restaurant, accompanied by lyric-driven music (aka a jingle) featuring one of the restaurant's most popular menu items — baby back ribs.

I was so embarrassed by the situation we found ourselves in that rather than give the assignment to anyone in my creative department, I decided to just do it myself. I sat down at my desk, and approximately three minutes later I had written the Chili's baby back ribs song.

To this day, I don't know why that song came to me so quickly or, on top of that, how it eventually ended up being sung by a character called "Fat Bastard" in the second *Austin Powers* movie. (Eventually, it showed up on every TV show from *Saturday Night Live* and *Will & Grace* to *Scrubs* and *The Daily Show with Jon Stewart.* To add insult to injury, *Advertising Age* named it the number one earworm of the decade.)

I'm also more than a little embarrassed that I had anything to do with it. For years, when the song came up in Chili's focus groups, one of two comments followed. "That's my favorite jingle." And, "If I hear that song one more time, I'm going to stick a fork in my eye."

The point is, I needed a music-driven television concept, and when I sat down to come up with one, that's what was there. Apparently, the same thing happened to Bob Dylan — with infinitely more impressive results — when he wrote "Like A Rolling Stone." There are times when everything is fully formed and just pops out.

If any aspect of the creative process is responsible for the broad misconception of how creativity works and, by association, who's creative and who isn't, this peculiar phenomenon is it.

Most creative solutions do not, abracadabra, drop onto our laps the second we snap our synapses. Creating can be a great deal of fun, but it usually requires significant effort — not "work" in the sense that it's unpleasant and leaves us wishing for more three-day weekends.

Creativity is "work" from the standpoint of quantity.

If creativity is about stumbling onto the answer, the path to creative brilliance requires a lot of "What-ifs." What if we did this? What if we did that? What if we did something else entirely? What if, what if, what if?

The more "What-ifs," the better the odds that one of them is going to be a "That's it!"

That means quantity first and exploring as many potential answers as possible. Or, as Ernest Hemingway reportedly said, "Write drunk. Edit sober."

Chapter 4

Setting the stage.

It's been said before, it's true and, for the most part, it's never been a terribly helpful piece of advice: "The best way to come up with an idea is to let the idea come to you."

Let's start with what that does *not* mean.

"Letting the idea come to you" is not a directive to sit, pen in hand, paper at a right angle, waiting for some sort of divine intervention, some metaphysical tap on the shoulder accompanied by a voice from above echoing, "Here it is. Go make your million dollars now."

It simply means that ideas can't be forced.

Paradoxically, the harder a person tries to come up with an idea, the less likely it is that he or she will. I wish it didn't work that way. I wish that hard work, as we traditionally understand it, led directly to creative breakthroughs. Everything we've been taught about everything else would suggest that it should.

But as stated earlier, we're not making widgets here.

We're not following logic trails.

Get out your tattoo pens again:

Stumbling onto an idea begins with setting the stage for it.

In her book *The Artist's Way*, Julia Cameron suggests that artists start their day by writing three pages of whatever comes to mind. No stopping to contemplate direction. Just three pages of stream-of-thought writing.

She calls this exercise "morning pages," and its purpose, basically, is to provide a level of clarity that typically circumvents the conscious mind. However, the benefits of putting pen to paper in this manner go beyond personal insights. (It's amazing what's already in our heads waiting to be discovered.)

Just writing is perhaps the simplest way to start the creative process. Want to write a short story but don't have a theme or storyline? Trying to come up with an idea for a book may be the worst possible way to do so. Instead, begin the process by writing anything at all and nothing in particular. It may not take more than a few pages for the idea to reveal itself.

Setting the stage for ideas by writing applies equally to non-artistic pursuits. Looking for a way to make solar panels more efficient? To reinvent air travel? To rethink how we educate our children.

Write without stopping, thinking or trying. If it helps, start with a random "What-if." What began as nothing more than a curious musing may very well lead to something that, if not crystal clear, is on the path to crystal clear.

As unconventional as that sounds, recording one's inner ramblings in order to rendezvous with serendipity doesn't come without some logic.

When writing isn't deliberate, the results are unexpected. When the results are unexpected, the final product is a surprise — and surprise shares a room with "Look what I found." (More about the role of surprise in the next chapter.)

I once gave my students an assignment that required everyone to write whatever came to mind for 30 seconds. Like morning pages, the only way they could mess up was to stop and think about what they were going to write. After 30 seconds, I asked them to stop and switch papers with the person next to them, read what he or she had written and then write for another 30 seconds, extending the story in whatever direction their thoughts took them.

To make it more interesting, I gave half the class the first line "Suddenly the door slammed." I asked the other half to start with the line "She always loved tea in the morning." After several more "write and switch" directives, the results were enlightening, to say the least. The students had no idea how they came up with the storylines that spilled out of their pens that day, and walked out of class a little bit stunned at what they had done and, apparently, were capable of doing again.

Playtime

The mental shift experienced when duplicating squiggly lines also occurs with the writing exercise just described — with the added bonus of having something more interesting than two squiggly lines when finished.

More important, it opens the mind to what it can do when it isn't trying to do anything in particular.

Take out a piece of paper and write down "The last thing Jamie needed was another piece of good news." No, that's not the sort of sentence most people would write. Yes, that's the point.

Starting from an unfamiliar place always sets the stage for an interesting journey. Beginning with that sentence, write for one minute *without stopping,* and most importantly, *without thinking* — letting whatever words that come to mind just spill out.

Creativity is about unplanned discovery. Just writing facilitates that. Do it. Be amazed.

Chapter 5

Imagine there's no reason.

Years ago, David Letterman started his monologue with the question, "Do you ever find yourself sitting around thinking, 'What if we shaved the dog, rubbed some tanning lotion on him and stuck him under a sun lamp?'?"

When it comes to getting ideas flowing, it's hard to beat questions like that. What if we constructed a skyscraper out of ping-pong balls? What if we replaced the tires on our cars with penguins? What if we built a giant magnifying glass?

Oddly enough, a very logical reason exists for exploring the ridiculous to uncover the brilliant.

Part of the brain's job description is to make sense out of nonsense. No matter how absurd the premise, our mind's first compulsion is to deliver a reasonable explanation of what's in front of it. That's why a rational approach to problem solving that begins with the expected tends to end with the predictable. Logic and reason have a bias towards familiar and known.

A totally unconventional supposition forces the mind to play with it, come to terms with it and, in the pursuit of a solution that makes sense, stumble onto something unexpected and potentially extraordinary.

It's like this.

The creative process is about going where no one has gone. As such, those first steps into the unknown, by definition, have to be strange and unfamiliar. It's only when everything starts making sense in a way it never has before — at the end of the process — that the idea is born.

Ask rational questions that define purpose, clarify issues, address target audiences and so on before the creative journey commences.

Once the quest for a creative solution begins, however, that's the time to take an uncharted turn into an alternate reality, ask a "What-if" that no one in his or her right mind would ask and then pursue an answer to that question as if it was every bit as legitimate as any logical one. (Think Alice's Wonderland, Superman's Bizarro World and living with teenage daughters.)

It's all about surprise.

By its very nature, any new thoughts that result from a creative quest are going to be a surprise. (The creative process is as much about surprising oneself as it is about coming up with fresh solutions.)

When was the last time a grocery store layout surprised anyone? How about a bank? Car dealership? Big-box store? Or Las Vegas, for that matter? (Same formula, different themes.)

A well-known advertising agency used to preach the mantra, "When everyone else zigs, zag." Why not design grocery stores with circular aisles and rotating shelves that bring the food to the shoppers? Why not remove the teller window barrier between bankers and customers? In fact, why not replace bank "tellers" with bank "listeners"? Why not replace showroom floors in car dealerships with virtual-reality rooms that provide customers with simulated driving experiences via a pair of smart goggles?

The answers to all these questions may be very logical that-would-never-work-in-a-million-years reasons. But that's not the point. The point is to give the mind permission to roam new territory. The entire playing field changes with that-would-never-work, no-one-would-ever-do-that "What-ifs."

More accurately, a new path is created — a path that leads where old paths can't. Continue down that road regardless of the brain's internal naysayers and logic police. That's where something so obvious it boggles the mind that no one thought of it before is just waiting to be discovered.

Chapter 6

The cat says "moo."

Cats don't say "moo." People do not attach feathers to their skin in order to fly. Elephants do not have valves protruding from the tops of their trunks that allow them to play sounds like a trumpet.

If creative people go to one well more often than others in their exploration of the ridiculous, it's juxtaposition. It's asking "What if we took this one thing and introduced it to this totally unrelated thing?" Most of the time, the answer is an obvious, and often entertaining, "Because that's just stupid." However, it only takes one time for it to make sense in a way that nothing else before it has.

It worked for nylon filament when it became a new way to trim weeds. It worked for balloons when they became a way to cushion drivers in automobile collisions. It worked for slingshots when they became a method for catapulting disgruntled birds into animated pigs.

In the restaurant industry, juxtaposition is practically a mantra. Cuisines from one country are constantly being "influenced" by ingredients and techniques used in another country. Ever wonder what would happen if someone crossed sushi with a burrito? Next trip to San Francisco look up a place called Sushirrito. (There's usually a line out the door.)

In his book *A Technique for Producing Ideas*, James Webb Young defines an idea as "a new combination of old elements." Introducing two unrelated items to create a sum greater than the whole is the basis for the creative process and why "What-ifs" eventually change everything.

The only thing ideas ask of their recipients is that they be tuned in to receive any thoughts, no matter how raw and unformed, at any moment. Creative solutions don't come to people in the shower because they bring their laptops in there with them. Ideas drop in like uninvited guests all the time.

Pay attention to those cosmic flirtations that come and go like high school romances and never get a second date because we're off to attend the next meeting, pick up carpool, see if that tuna salad in the back of the refrigerator is still good.

Maybe those ideas will come back. Maybe they won't.

Chapter 7

Sometimes everyone has the answer but you.

How would Captain Kirk do it? How would your mom do it? How would a sightless person do it?

Imagining how someone else would solve a problem creates new paths for discovery.

How would SpongeBob solve traffic congestion in big cities? How would the scarecrow from the *Wizard of Oz* do it? How about Tarzan?

SpongeBob, who seems to stroll down a lot of streets for a sea creature, might suggest floating roadways that activate like moving sidewalks when traffic slows so that cars never come to a stop. The scarecrow might lobby for putting computer "brains" in cars that override drivers' decisions on congested roads. Tarzan might consider eliminating vehicles altogether and transporting people via a system of elevated vacuum tubes.

The point is that any subject, any problem, has a multitude of answers — most of them unworkable, but all with the potential to lead to the next brilliant solution.

Given the willingness of the seeker to seek.

Playtime

I hesitate to suggest this, because no creative person I've ever known set out to create something in such a deliberate way, but if it helps, write down a problem in one column. Then, write down ten totally unrelated things in another column — such as the color pink, an aardvark, nerds, something found on a farm, Martians, famous paintings, plots from horror movies, etc. Then ask questions like, "How might one solve this problem using the color pink? How would a nerd solve it? How might one solve it using vegetables?"

In essence, that's how the creative brain works. It just doesn't ordinarily do so in such a deliberate way. Again, it's all about discovery. 1. Toss out "What-ifs." 2. Stumble onto "Ahas!" — something so unique, so funny, so unexpected, so perfect that it makes sense like nothing else before it.

Chapter 8

To get to the other side.

As a young advertising copywriter, I often hung out with carbon copies of myself. (Note to anyone under 50: a carbon copy was the predecessor of the photocopy.) Which means that on occasion, several of us would get together over drinks to talk about how stupid everybody in our industry was except us.

On one of these occasions, a fellow copywriter asked me about a funny radio spot I had written and produced that was getting some positive buzz. He wanted to know how the idea came to me. "Actually," I told him, "I wrote the punch line first, then came up with a storyline to go with it."

To see his face, I might as well have told him that I sold his sister. The revelation that it was perfectly fine to start with "Z" and work back to "A" never occurred to him.

Creating is more about breaking rules than following them. And it applies just as equally to coming up with the next digital sensation as it does to writing the next blockbuster.

Take cell phones. Before Apple created the iPhone, handsets were considered worthless commodities that existed as little more than vehicles to get users to a carrier's network. Apple flipped that thinking on its head by making the phone the most important thing.

Take John Irving. He writes the last sentence of his novels first — including character names and how the story resolves. Once he's written that sentence, he creates a story to go with it.

Looking for the next "wish-I'd-thought-of-that" idea? Design the app's icon, and then decide its function. Let the colors determine the subject matter of the painting. Rethink education so that kids do their homework first (at school) and their class work last (at home).

Oh, wait. The acclaimed Kahn Academy already did that last one.

Start backward. Fill in the blanks. Create something no one has ever seen or heard.

Chapter 9

Get the picture.

Given our inclination to start every project with pen, paper or keyboard, it's only natural at the first stage of addressing a creative challenge to begin with words.

But writing isn't the only way to stumble onto ideas. Draw. Even if it's stick figures, sketch out visual solutions to the problem. It's not for display in a museum. No one else is going to see it. As long as the creator recognizes it, that's all that matters.

Or, as long as that keyboard is there, type a few words into a search engine. Only instead of going to articles, go to images.

Look at photos. Illustrations. Graphics. Seek out visual representations of the problem in front of you. Mash a couple of the photos together. Extend, subtract, embellish, play. Look for connections.

Starting with an image more often than not results in a direction that words alone would never suggest. One of the best ways to come up with an idea for a screenplay, for example, is to start with the casting. If the story doesn't write itself, knowing what the characters look like will, at the very least, suggest a direction or a genre.

One of the most enlightening things I learned working with art directors and designers is that when the visual for an advertising concept is determined up front, the words often write themselves.

I was once assigned to create an ad for a financial institution. The point of the ad was to acknowledge that while the state of the economy was improving, it still had a way to go towards reaching a full recovery. Among the visual images the art director suggested was an empty railroad tunnel with tracks in the foreground. I couldn't write the headline fast enough: "The light at the end of the tunnel isn't a train. But it's not Tinker Bell either."

So get the picture. Then write to it.

Chapter 10

Connecting the dots that aren't there.

Steve Jobs once defined creativity as connecting the dots — not the dots that logically link to each other, but the ones that no one ever thought to link.

Again, we're back to the "What-ifs." What if we wanted to rethink the ladder? What's the biggest problem with ladders? People fall off. Why do they fall off? Usually it's because the ladder is placed on an uneven surface, and when the ladder starts to tip, the climber tips with it. So, what if we set a carpenter's level (that sealed glass tube partially filled with liquid containing an air bubble whose position reveals how level a surface is) on the bottom step of the ladder and then attached adjustable rubber "feet" to the legs — like on a tripod? What if we take something that people expect on a tripod — because if a tripod isn't level, the photos from the camera attached to it won't be either — and adapt it to a ladder? Make a connection that seems obvious only after someone comes up with it. (Disclaimer: I'm guessing I'm not the first person to think of this adjustable ladder thing, so if by chance I am, feel free to get the ball rolling and make a gazillion dollars for us.)

A Silicon Valley company called Nest recently applied

this very sort of thinking to the thermostat — another product everyone has seen a thousand times without giving it a second glance. Taking design cues from the iPod and introducing digital capabilities more commonly associated with high-tech devices, Nest turned the lowly thermostat into something almost magical. (Note: In the history of the world, no one has ever described a thermostat as "magical.") After finding success there, they brought the same let's-create-a-better-one thinking to another overlooked commodity in the house: smoke detectors. It's as if their marketing plan is to go into The Home Depot and take inventory of what products could benefit from an aesthetic rethink and tech injection. (Their genius hasn't gone unnoticed. Google recently purchased them for $3.2 billion. In cash.)

Getting back to Mr. Jobs, there's one more thing he said about creative people and their innate ability to find connections.

Creative people notice things that most people take for granted. They are observers. They notice how some people walk on the balls of their feet and spring upward while others stride heel to toe. They notice how letters on a sign are often spaced unevenly and, as a result, affect how the words can be read. They notice the way dogs use their ears to express emotions.

Listen to conversations. Watch how people use their eyebrows. Notice how food is arranged on a plate at fine restaurants. Observe how cars match the personalities of their drivers.

Aside from often using this knowledge to be incredibly annoying, insensitive or belittling, creative people use these observations to make unexpected connections. They notice everything. And some day, some way, they find a way to use it.

Some people like to keep a journal of interesting things they come across. Others, in this age of the smart phone, take pictures. Having a system of storage and retrieval is helpful for a number of reasons — not the least of which is establishing a habit that could payoff huge dividends at some point down the line.

So, don't just look. See.

Playtime

Rethink something everyone has seen a thousand times and never given a second glance. Take the paintbrush. What's the biggest problem with paintbrushes? Getting the paint to go exactly where you want it? Drips? Cleaning? Comfort? You decide. Then fix it.

Starting again with pen and paper, write without stopping, just like the earlier writing exercise, letting each statement suggest the next without regard to whether it's directly related to the problem or not.

(Hint: Question everything. Does a brush have to have bristles? Would it be better if the handle was a foot longer? Should it be disposable and degradable?)

You'll know when to stop.

Chapter 11

Get a life.

A number of companies think the best way to get the most out of their people is to work them long hours. At some ad agencies, they have a saying: "If you don't come in on Saturday, don't bother coming in on Sunday."

Working this way is incredibly shortsighted. Here's why.

First, the obvious: consistently working people long hours burns them out. Creative productivity, in particular, diminishes when employees are put in the position of drawing from a well that isn't regularly being replenished.

Creativity is enhanced when people with different experiences interact and, as a result, stumble upon new connections. When employees don't have significant lives outside the office, their creative babies slowly become the victims of inbreeding. Everyone's abilities to draw on new experiences shrink, and fresh eventually gives way to familiar.

Cousins don't marry cousins for a reason. Only by

getting out in the world and having new adventures, exploits and relationships are people in a position to escort new thoughts to the table.

Once again: Ideas are basically about bringing together two diverse things and seeing how they interact. The more opportunities people have to experience different things, the greater the potential for new ideas. Working 60-hour weeks, day after day, year after year with the same people is not a recipe for fresh or new.

It doesn't do much for productivity in general either. Consider the Greeks. They clock in over 600 more hours a year on the job than the Germans do, yet the Germans are 70% more productive. (GDP per hour worked.)

Finally, there's percolation. Often it's necessary to stop the process and do something else entirely in order to give the idea time to form, i.e., let the subconscious earn its keep. Go to Starbucks. Shoot some hoops. Focusing on a completely different project or area doesn't mean the brain has stopped working on the problem — which is why answers have a way of showing up when least expected.

As a designer friend once told me, "It's pretty much the Zen thing. You don't see the solution until you turn your back on the problem."

So, get out of the office. Go places. Do things. And don't check e-mail every ten minutes. To be valuable to a company, get away from it. To create something new, stop working on it.

Chapter 12

Is that an idea in your pocket?

It's time to address the elephant with the fluorescent tusks in the room: brainstorming.

A group of people gather together to share their thoughts. All thoughts, regardless of how wild and crazy, are not only valid, but encouraged. With each thought, an opportunity exists to build on the other. At the end of the session, "Voila!" — new ideas everywhere.

The only problem with brainstorming is that if its purpose is to deliver breakthroughs, the overwhelming majority of the time, it doesn't work. And the main reason it doesn't work is the same reason that it should — the requisite to throw out any thought, no matter how ridiculous.

People are rarely comfortable enough — or secure enough — to share any random fragment that pops into their heads. Human beings spend an inordinate amount of their lives trying to impress each other and even more time trying to look good in front of their supervisors. Asking them to suspend sounding smart and responsible for 30 minutes in order to contribute the kind of unconventional musings required to uncover unexpected solutions is almost impossible.

As a result, brainstorming sessions become a charade of half-hearted "What-ifs" that sound invariably like every idea everyone has already heard. Occasionally, someone blurts out an uncharacteristic thought that gets a laugh, and the lesson everyone learns is not to be that person.

(Research recently uncovered a number of other reasons why brainstorming sessions generally disappoint. The rule that forbids criticism inhibits collaboration. Extroverts dominate. Plus, some people are simply unproductive working in a group structure.)

The process of building on one thought to find another is the cornerstone of the creative process. Advertising agencies are organized into copywriter and art director teams for this very reason. But, it often takes time for a new team to become comfortable enough with each other to share their oddest deliberations without fear of being judged negatively. It's only after the relationship is established that the partners become productive.

So, it's not the idea of brainstorming that's invalid. It's that unless and until people have established a working relationship that allows them to come off like complete idiots in front of each other, they can't adhere to brainstorming's most vital tenet: The more outlandish the thought — and the more willingness to play off that thought — the better.

Playtime

One way to try to circumvent the reluctance of looking IQ-challenged in front of associates and peers is to make "stupidity" the objective. Start an assignment with the ten worst ways to solve the problem. If the idea isn't dumb enough, it doesn't get written down.

What usually happens is that after a while, finding the next really bad idea is extremely difficult, and truly awful thoughts open paths to totally fresh ones.

It's not unlike rule number nine of Pixar's 22 rules of storytelling: "When you're stuck, make a list of what WOULDN'T happen next. Lots of times the material to get you unstuck will show up."

It all gets back to that fine line between dumb and smart. When it comes to the creative process, beginning the journey with "dumb" is not so much about hopping on the bus and looking for the express lane to "smart" as it is going along for the ride and realizing that "smart" just made a beeline for the bus.

Chapter 13

Copycats.

Sir Isaac Newton once said, "If I have seen further than others, it is by standing on the shoulders of giants."

There's no need to start from scratch when a separate body of work is just begging for someone to build on it. Look at what's been done before. Take it to another level.

There's an online video series called "Everything is a Remix." In it, the writer and producer, Kirby Ferguson, does a fascinating job examining the concept of originality as it applies to creators and their creations.

The idea for the first Macintosh computer started with a not-coincidentally similar project at Xerox that Steve Jobs just happened to see and then liberally borrowed from as the basis for an entirely new operating system. Led Zeppelin was successful for a number of reasons. Writing songs that were uncomfortably close to other artists' work was one of them.

But with apologies to Ferguson, everything is not a remix.

At some point, an idea has to have a beginning. It has to start somewhere, even if it was influenced by something completely unrelated and, thus, not so much a remix as a new connection. Why didn't the original inventor or artist receive the fame and fortune that followed for the people who took those initial ideas one or two steps further? The original creation may have been too crude to succeed or had no audience to appreciate it or not enough support behind it. The time may not have been right, and so on.

The point is, the basis for an idea may already be out there. Build on it. Fix it. Adapt it to fit your needs.

Do NOT outright steal it. Do not simply put a coat of paint on it and call it new. Do not confuse a remix with a new idea. **An idea isn't new unless something *significant* has been introduced to the equation.**

None of this is to say that on occasion, some value or justifiable purpose doesn't exist for a remix. Sometimes, doing a remix is not only perfectly fine, but preferable. The only caveat is that when trekking into grey areas of ownership, always be cognizant of ethical (and legal) lines, and give credit where credit is due.

An idea influenced by something somewhere else isn't plagiarism. An idea so close to the original execution that the difference is academic is.

Some of the world's most celebrated creative ideas began as totally unrelated observations. That's not only as it should be, it's one of those connections that serves as the basis for creative thought. Henry Ford began experimenting with the idea of the assembly line only after one of his managers told him about a visit to a Chicago slaughterhouse where he observed pigs being "disassembled" along conveyor belts.

The framing for the next big idea is out there waiting for someone to build a new wing. Find it. Uncover it. Use it as a springboard to something else entirely.

Or, as Sir Isaac might have said (but didn't): "Find yourself a giant. Then ask for a piggyback."

Chapter 14

The genius of Curious George.

If creative people have one trait that trumps all others, it's curiosity. Not just about how things work. Or what's behind door number three.

They have a curiosity for life — the kind of curiosity that enriches life experiences. Nothing fills the well like being there and doing that. (Comfort zones are way overrated.)

Travel to unfamiliar places and experience them beyond tourist attractions. Go to an exhibit unrelated to any personal interests. Talk to strangers, despite what your mother told you.

Do all of the above without judgment or preconceptions. Go into it not as a means to any particular end, but for the same reason George Mallory climbed Mount Everest: because it's there.

At some point, those experiences will provide the fodder for answers to future problems. More important, to use Helen Keller's words, "Life is either a daring adventure or nothing at all."

One more time: Ideas are basically the introduction of two elements that, before they became roommates, were doing just fine living in separate apartments. The more knowledge a person has from a wide variety of sources, the better equipped he or she is to create something new and fresh.

The necessity of drawing from a vast array of experiences and disciplines in order to find the elusive big idea makes a pretty compelling case for a liberal arts education. Not that there's anything wrong with majoring in business or engineering or law. It's just that to create, the broader the base of knowledge one has, the more opportunities to mix and match. Study cultural anthropology, English literature, a foreign language and the history of film. Someday, something from one of those disciplines will provide the missing link for an idea whose time has come.

Like the Henry Ford example in the last chapter, some of the world's greatest ideas came from taking a common practice or way of thinking from one industry or profession and applying it to another.

Great leaps forward aren't without their stepping stones.

Chapter 15

The road to nowhere leads somewhere.

What does non-linear thinking look like in practice?

Take a pesky little problem like world hunger. Between the creative person's ears, the thought process might go something like this:

Solve hunger problem, I like bananas, bananas are yellow, yellow means you're a coward, cowards run, running makes me sweat, there's nothing like a shower when you're sweaty, hot showers are best, global warming is making the world hotter, hot climates are going to have an impact on agriculture, farms may not be able to grow as much food, people may not be able to go to the grocery store and find everything they need, maybe they'll have to start growing some of their own food, people should grow more of their own food, if everybody had a vegetable garden, we'd have food left over, if we had food left over we could give it to people who don't have enough...

Now, imagine doing this ten more times and arriving at ten different conclusions.

That's how the search for new solutions works in the

heads of people who don't give much thought to processes. (Sidebar: Before beginning any creative endeavor, it helps to have a deeper understanding of the subject than I displayed here.)

Hop on a train of thought. Take it for a ride. Get off. Hop on the next one.

Chapter 16

When your baby is a monkey.

Sometimes, the best ideas turn out to be the worst ideas, and the lesson everybody learns from those moments is never to let them happen again.

Unfortunately, while failure is often painful, it's also essential to the breakthroughs that provide creative thinking's biggest rewards.

Avoiding failure means avoiding risk. Seeking safe routes. Taking proven paths. As such, the output of any effort is going to be familiar and limited. (It's certainly not going to blow any minds, gain throngs of admirers or make the cover of any magazines.)

Failure is integral to the creative process. It's going to happen. When it does, correct the course and get on with it. Don't let the fear of failing slow the journey or worse, keep it from ever getting off the ground.

Worry more about not trying something just because no one has done it before.

That said, accepting failure is not an endorsement for

moving forward without forethought. Think things out. Take deliberate steps aimed at achieving specific goals. Learn from the mistakes of others.

Just remember that being smart isn't the same thing as waiting for the myth of certainty to act. Embrace the eventuality of failures along the way or any explorations into the unknown will be timid at best, and any victories will be small or meaningless at worst.

Failure in the pursuit of a creative solution is a gift. It's like getting the instruction manual after the botched first attempt at assembling the bike. It's information that wasn't available earlier. It's the basis for new insight.

Failure does not mean that introducing what turned out to be a bad idea was a mistake. It just means it's not easy.

It just means the journey isn't over.

Chapter 17

What's so great about that?

Finally, just as important as creating ideas are the people in a position to judge them. A lot of creative output goes nowhere because it couldn't get past someone whose idea of creativity is restroom signage that reads "Jack" and "Jill."

The results of creative expression are fragile. A lot of shepherding is necessary if an idea is going to survive. Equally important to the delivery and implementation of new thoughts are people in charge who have some idea of what qualifies as a good idea and what doesn't.

That starts with having something as simple as a standard. For example, it's amazing how often people and companies put the word "great" in mission statements, yet never take the time to define exactly what "great" means. (Ask around. It means significantly different things to different people.)

Clear, concise definitions are vital for a number of reasons, not the least of which is that in any creative endeavor, you're not done until you're done. And there's no way of knowing when you're done until you have some idea of what done looks like.

I was once tasked with defining "great creative" as part of a new business presentation at a major advertising agency. After spending several days and way too many words qualifying every nuance of how I thought we should define, interpret and understand "great," one of our account guys asked to see my thoughts.

I showed him the four pages I had written. He shook his head and said, "You know what great creative is? Great creative is when people can't stop talking about what you did."

Talk about an epiphany. So I went back and found my own words.

"Great creative does the job. And then some."

Chapter 18

The disclaimer chapter.

Typically, the introduction of creative ideas is followed by a chorus of "We could never do that"s. (Or the equally popular "The client will never buy that"s.)

Coming up with something creative is the easy part compared to actually selling it. People are not comfortable with different. They like safe. They understand tried and true. They preach, "There's a reason everybody does it this way. Because it works."

So what's the point of all this creativity stuff anyway?

To a creative person, that's sort of like asking, "What's the point of all this breathing stuff anyway?" Creative people exist to solve problems. Hand them a solution and one of two things happens. They totally rethink the assignment and come back with something else entirely. Or, disgruntled, they deliver a half-hearted replica of the mandated answer.

(Sidebar: Telling a creative person or entity what to do or how to do it is a recipe for frustration and disappointment. Wrong way: "Solve this problem this way." Right way: "Here's a problem. Bring me some solutions.")

For most everyone else, creativity is the path of last resort. It's for when the what-works-today-works-incrementally-less-well-tomorrow dilemma reaches a tipping point that can no longer be ignored.

It's like this.

Most people execute to a standard. That's who they are. That's what they do. At the end of the day, the work gets done. Nobody goes away overly impressed, but then that wasn't the point. The shelves were stocked. The mail was delivered. The cavity was filled.

For the majority of people, the upside of personal performance is based on things like time, volume, service, attitude and money. Was the task accomplished when expected — or better yet, sooner than expected? Did the product meet expectations? Did service exceed expectations? Did we make a decent profit? Etcetera.

As long as supply and demand line up, nobody gives it a second thought.

Delivering at a creative level is different. The best creative people are fueled by a drive to reimagine or rethink something for the better — to put "good" on the line, if necessary, for the possibility of achieving "great."

As such, if there's any bottom line to the creative process, it's this:

The key to creative success is an unwavering commitment to delivering at a higher level — *because way too many plausible and even positive options exist to justify giving up and settling for the status quo along the way.*

If people who deliver great creative work live by any creed, it's that there is no such thing as good enough.

People and companies that deliver great creative ideas time after time do so not just because they are talented but because they are tenacious. They don't give up. They aren't willing to settle for less because less simply isn't an option. They refuse to surrender until they surprise everyone with their answers, including themselves.

They get knocked down. They get back up.

There are reasons why the work that people and companies do isn't as good as the work they want to do, hope to do or are capable of doing. Good reasons. Valid reasons. Sometimes even irrefutable reasons.

But, to those committed to delivering great creative solutions, reasons are excuses for failing, and excuses are for making people feel better about delivering average work.

Anyone can produce a gas station that looks like every other gas station and, given its location and market, makes a decent profit. But, just like all those companies making cell phones when Apple decided to make one of its own, the company whose identity and existence are based on delivering at a creative level is the company that eventually sets the bar for everyone else.

The upside of what creativity brings to a company knows no limits. Yes, choosing a creative path can be risky. Yes, sometimes it means failure. But it's less risky than producing the same products and services everybody else is producing in a marketplace that rarely rewards the companies sitting on the third or fourth rung of the ladder in their respective categories like it does the top two.

Just ask BlackBerry, JCPenney and RC Cola.

Chapter 19

A final thought.

In virtually every business category, a high level of parity exists. For the most part, the people who staff advertising agencies, engineering companies, accounting/law/brokerage firms, digital startups and so on are smart, capable and driven to succeed. Compelling personalities and cultural differences occasionally give one company the edge over another. But typically, businesses chase the same markets the same way with the same caliber of people.

And the go-to, not-so-secret weapon they use to compete is "working harder."

Our infatuation with sports and their accompanying metaphors is partly to blame for this mindset. Since the first ball was put into play on the first court, field or course, the lesson has been that superior effort delivers superior results, i.e., victory.

It works in football. It works in baseball. It works in basketball. It causes businesses to make a lot of questionable decisions.

Hard work is essential. (Duh!) Unfortunately,

particularly here in America where the Puritan work ethic is so ingrained in our national psyche that it feels heretical to even question it, hard work has become a false god. *Hard work has become proxy for value.*

Sometimes hard work and value line up. Most of the time, the two aren't even in the same building.

In the business world, competition in any given category only serves to force everyone to share an ever-decreasing slice of the same pie. As PayPal billionaire Peter Thiel noted, in baseball, if a team is down ten runs in the eighth inning, it has no choice but to do everything it can to score eleven runs in the ninth. If a business, on the other hand, is consistently having trouble making its numbers, it has an option that ballplayers don't.

It can change the game.

Instead, the choice that businesses and individuals make when they find themselves in situations where they have no distinct advantage is to invest even more of themselves into what they are doing. They don't realize they're in a hole, so their solution is to keep digging.

Everybody can't win (succeed) when everybody is playing the same game (business) in the same league (market) with only so many fans that have the means to buy tickets (customers/clients). No wonder, in economic terms, the definition of pure competition is a situation where nobody makes any money. (Whereas capitalism is all about making money.)

So how does a business stand out, break out, win out? How do individuals succeed beyond all expectations? The companies and people who rise to the top don't necessarily do so because they compete to be the best in the world at what they do. They do so because at some point they have the clarity to pursue a vision that sets them apart — that makes them the *only* ones in the world at what they do.

In the arts, we observe this all the time. Elvis Presley wasn't like anyone else in the world. For that matter, neither is Elvis Costello. Critically lauded rapper Eminem is not like critically lauded rapper Kanye West. Matisse did not compete with Picasso who did not compete with van Gogh. Each brought a completely unique view to his art. In architecture, Frank Lloyd Wright rose to the top of his field not just because he worked hard, but because he had a perspective that captured the imagination. No one is like Meryl Streep, Madonna or Tina Fey.

In business, naming companies that have redefined their categories with a unique point of view or vision isn't quite as easy. Apple always comes to mind for obvious reasons. Dell, rarely, if ever. But, interestingly, the reason Dell was once the darling of the stock market set was because it was founded on the unique (at the time) premise that personal computers were a commodity and, as such, could be differentiated by how they were configured and then sold through the mail. Had the world not changed, Dell would still be making money hand over fist. Unfortunately, Dell's first idea was its last idea, and over the years, it has become just one more former computer company struggling to find a compelling reason for being.

Today, we are asking people and businesses to play games they cannot win, and to do so they are reverting to the only thing they know how to do — working harder to get a bigger share of a shrinking pie — when what they should be doing is changing the game.

And the whole point of creativity is to change the game.

Just ask PayPal, Tesla Motors and Amazon.

Chapter 20

Excellence =
Medium **x** Creativity Squared.

Albert Einstein knew a thing or two about where ideas come from. Here are three totally counterintuitive things he said that hopefully make a bit more sense now.

1. Creativity is the residue of wasted time.

2. If at first the idea is not absurd, then there's no hope for it.

3. Imagination is more important than science.

Einstein tells you "What." This book is all about "How." But to succeed in any creative endeavor, the most important question is, "Why?"

(Hint: The answer is in your bones.)

Epilogue

In the first *Toy Story* movie, Sheriff Woody is unconvinced that Buzz Lightyear can fly. (He can't.) In his attempt to prove otherwise, Buzz jumps off Andy's bed into what quickly becomes a freefall, before he serendipitously lands on a rubber ball that bounces him onto a racecar that propels him via racetrack loop back in the air, where he latches onto a toy plane attached to the ceiling, and spins around the room a few times before landing with a 360-degree "dismount" back on the bed.

Stunned and desperate to save face in front of the other toys, Woody proclaims Buzz's feat to be "Falling. With style."

Falling with style may be as good a metaphor for the creative process as there is: jumping off into the unknown in search of a perfect landing somewhere as yet to be determined.

More important, the lesson here is that nothing happens without the leap.

So, leap.

Notes

Introduction

With regards to pop culture's fondness for oversimplification — in this case, by assigning exclusive functions to one brain hemisphere or the other —, my introduction to the subject (based on Dr. Roger Sperry's work with split-brain patients) came in an early edition of the Betty Edwards book, *Drawing on the Right Side of the Brain* (Tarcher/Putnam, May 1, 1989). As it relates to drawing, her book is beyond enlightening. Unfortunately, in the years since its publication, Ms. Edwards has been faulted for popularizing the whole right brain/left brain (creative side/logical side) dichotomy. According to the people who know these things (scientists), while the hemispheres may specialize, the two sides normally work together.

Also, the person who came up with the idea to mount those custom-designed skateboard decks was Brendan McKenna.

Chapter 2

I further have to credit Ms. Edwards as the inspiration behind the squiggly line exercise designed to give readers a feel for the mind shift that occurs during a creative endeavor. In *Drawing on the Right Side of the Brain,* she has readers replicate the classic face/vase illustration — where the profiles of two faces create the sides of a vase. But, basically, it's the same idea.

Chapter 3

Tom Faulkner produced the original Chili's baby back ribs song, enhancing it nicely along the way.

In *Keys to the Rain: The Definitive Bob Dylan Encyclopedia,* Oliver Trager quotes Bob Dylan as saying "It just came, you know," when describing how he wrote "Like a Rolling Stone" (Billboard Books, October 1, 2004). Dylan likened the experience to writing a long piece of "vomit."
http://en.wikipedia.org/wiki/Like_a_Rolling_Stone.

Plus, nobody knows for certain if Ernest Hemingway said "Write drunk. Edit sober." Other possible candidates include Peter De Vries, Dylan Thomas and Mark Twain.

Chapter 4

In addition to the concept of morning pages, *The Artist's Way* (Jeremy P. Tarcher/Putman, March 4, 2002) by Julia Cameron contains a number of other insights and exercises regarding the things creative people do to thwart their creativity, including ways to thwart the thwarting.

I'm not the first teacher to give students the tandem writing assignment described in this chapter — although I did put my own twist on it by having them start with thematically incongruent sentences. I first became aware of the exercise after reading about a mismatched pair of students, whose attempts to compose a story together produced one of the funniest miscarriages of writing I've ever seen.

Chapter 5

My contention that the brain exists to make sense out of nonsense is corroborated by a study done at the University of British Columbia. Check out an article in *The New York Times* from October 5, 2009, called "How Nonsense Sharpens the Intellect" by Benedict Carey for background.

Chapter 6

While James Webb Young's book, *A Technique for Producing Ideas* (Waking Lion Press, July 22, 2009), only scratches the surface of the creative process, it's still a great practical read on the subject and provides an easy entry level introduction to a creative technique that anyone looking to expand their way of thinking can access.

Chapter 7

The idea of making lists that can be mixed and matched randomly to produce an unexpected result is a fairly common exercise. Apparently, even Leonardo da Vinci did it.
http://creativethinking.net/DT08_DaVincisIdeabox.htm?Entry=Good

Chapter 9

The art director responsible for coming up with the train tunnel visual was the same Brendan McKenna who came up with the idea for the mounted skateboard decks.

Chapter 11

More and more seems to be written every day regarding the downsides of working an inordinate number of hours. The bottom line that continues to assert itself is that working longer makes people less productive, effective and creative. A quick synopsis on this topic (along with a nice graph that supports the Greek and German productivity numbers cited in this chapter) can be found in an article entitled "Get A Life" from *The Economist* (September 24, 2013).

With regards to getting away from a task so that the subconscious can bring something to the party (also known as percolation or incubation), Leslie Berlin provides a bit more depth on this phenomenon in *The*

New York Times: "We'll Fill This Space, But First A Nap." (September 27, 2008)

A credit goes to Ken Shafer, who also designed the cover of this book, for the quote regarding "the Zen thing."

Chapter 12

Research confirming the problems with brainstorming seems to be all over the place these days. And that's the problem. Finding a one-stop summation of the latest brainstorming fallacies isn't easy. However, a brief synopsis can be found in an article headlined "Why Brainstorming Doesn't Improve Productivity or Creativity" by Ray Williams in *Psychology Today* (April 10, 2012).

Regarding Pixar's 22 rules of storytelling, the other 21 rules are just as fascinating. Find them on the web.

Chapter 13

While I have issues with Kirby Ferguson's web series, "Everything is a Remix," it is extremely well done and worth viewing. Find it at http://everythingisaremix.info/watch-the-series. If nothing else, Ferguson establishes the role that influence plays in the creative process.

The part in this chapter about Henry Ford coming up

with the idea for the assembly line based on a visit to a slaughterhouse is corroborated in his 1922 book, *My Life and Work* (CreateSpace Independent Publishing Platform, November 25, 2013), where he is quoted as saying "The idea came in a general way from the overhead trolley that the Chicago packers use in dressing beef."

Chapter 14

With regards to my comments in favor of a liberal arts education, my personal lament here is that most colleges have lost their way. For what society has rationalized are both practical and economic reasons, too many institutions have become very expensive trade schools. If there is any lesson to be gleaned from this book, it's that the focus on specialization makes students less capable of turning what they know into something new and fresh, i.e. interesting and creative. Money makes terrible decisions.

Chapter 17

For the record, the account guy who inadvertently led me to a more succinct definition of great creative was Chuck Grady. Chuck always had an opinion. I'm glad he shared that one.

Chapter 19

On April 23, 2012, an article by David Brooks called "The Creative Monopoly" appeared in *The New York Times*. Based on a class being taught at Stanford University by PayPal founder Peter Thiel, the piece was so compelling that I tracked down the lecture notes to learn more. With gratitude to Blake Masters, the student who posted the notes (April 15, 2012), the impetus for the thinking in this chapter can be found here: http://blakemasters.com/post/21169325300/peter-thiels-cs183-startup-class-4-notes-essay.

Acknowledgements

In 1998, Drs. Patty Alvey and Deborah Morrison invited me to teach a course on creativity in the College of Communications at the University of Texas (Austin). I accepted without having a clue if what they were asking — teaching creativity — was even possible. Fortunately, and with their help, I somehow found the words that eventually provided the foundation for this book. A sincere thanks goes to them for that opportunity.

I'd also like to acknowledge the dozen or so people who took the time to read earlier versions of this book and provide their valuable feedback, most notably Stan Richards and Luke Sullivan. There aren't two guys on the planet who understand the creative process better than them. They could have easily said they were too busy. They didn't.

I can't begin to thank all of the incredibly talented art directors, designers and copywriters I've worked with over the years — people who taught me everything I know about creativity and made me better just for having worked with them. However, I have to recognize an early creative director/boss, Tom Poth, who told a much younger me after listening to my latest litany of excuses for delivering subpar creative concepts, "You know, at some point in your career, you're going to have to accept responsibility for the work you do." That advice/admonishment literally changed my life. Overnight, I went from playing the victim to learning what I needed to learn in order to do what I wanted to do. (That journey could be a book all by itself.)

A final shout-out goes to Steve Gurasich and Roy Spence, who taught me that being an entrepreneur means not being afraid to make a decision. (If it's wrong, just make another decision.) Along with Tim McClure and Judy Trabulsi, they gave me a national stage as executive creative director at GSD&M that eventually provided me with just enough credibility to write a book about creativity. Now that was a ride.

About the Cover

Credit for the cover design goes to Ken Shafer. A graduate of East Texas State University, Ken began his career in Dallas before moving to Seattle and establishing Ken Shafer Design. That was 25 years ago. Since then, he has created print collateral, publication designs and signature identities for an array of clients — including Nike, the NBA, the NFL, the PGA Tour, Microsoft, ABC, National Geographic and more. Tiger Woods wears one of Ken's designs on his hat. Ken has a wife and two children and maybe a little too much confidence when he dons a pair of inline skates. For more information, go to kenshaferdesign.com.

Made in the USA
San Bernardino, CA
24 October 2014